A PRACTICAL HANDBOOK FOR THE BOSS

A PRACTICAL HANDBOOK FOR THE BOSS

What Your Momma Tried to Teach You
about Playing Nicely with Others

Jim Willis

A Practical Handbook for the Boss
What Your Momma Tried to Teach You about Playing Nicely with Others

iUniverse books may be ordered through booksellers or by contacting:

iUniverse
1663 Liberty Drive
Bloomington, IN 47403
www.iuniverse.com
1-800-Authors (1-800-288-4677)

Because of the dynamic nature of the Internet, any web addresses or links contained in this book may have changed since publication and may no longer be valid. The views expressed in this work are solely those of the author and do not necessarily reflect the views of the publisher, and the publisher hereby disclaims any responsibility for them.

Any people depicted in stock imagery provided by Thinkstock are models, and such images are being used for illustrative purposes only.
Certain stock imagery © Thinkstock.

ISBN: 978-1-4917-6072-7 (sc)
ISBN: 978-1-4917-6074-1 (hc)
ISBN: 978-1-4917-6073-4 (e)

Print information available on the last page.

iUniverse rev. date: 02/09/2015

For my loving family:

Jan
Ryan
Caleta

Thank you for your love and encouragement throughout the years. I'm sorry for any time I was away taking care of business and missing any important events in your lives. I hope you are as proud of me as I am of each of you.

If you want to be successful, it's just this simple. Know what you are doing. Love what you are doing. And believe in what you are doing.

Will Rogers

CONTENTS

PREFACE

Since you picked this book up, I would guess that one of two things is going on: 1) you are an administrator / leader and you are looking for some ideas to do a better job or, 2) you want to become an administrator / leader and are looking for ideas to get you started on a successful career. Hopefully, you will find something in this handbook to spur those interests and ideas of your own to make your career more successful. What would I like for you to gain from reading this handbook? More than anything, that there are some new ideas within these pages that you have never before considered. There could also be some things that you have heard some place before, but have forgotten about or not bothered to put into practice at all. Mostly, I hope that you can pick up on some of my own successes and even some of my failures so you can learn from them.

For those of you who value credibility, let me introduce myself to you. I have worked in a variety of careers, beginning as a "slick-sleeved airman", and eventually being in an administrative position where I supervised seventy people. In other words, I have experienced being supervised and supervising from both ends of the spectrum.

After graduation from high school in 1971, I joined the United States Air Force and got out four years later as a staff sergeant. I did stay in the Air Force Reserves for the next nineteen years, where I eventually retired as a master sergeant.

The main reason I got out of active duty was to go to college, where I earned a BSEd in elementary education, a MSEd in reading, and certification above my masters in elementary administration. I spent thirteen years in an elementary classroom in two different districts, teaching every subject. I began my career in administration after that becoming an elementary school administrator, for thirteen years in a single school district in Southwest Oklahoma. Just like everyone else, I looked for the open position and competed with other people to show the superintendent and school board members that I was the best person for the job. There were many successes along the way in the form of state and federal recognition of our programs, an increase of nearly 100 percent in mandated national achievement test scores, and a dramatic decrease in disciplinary problems within our school. I give the credit for those improvements to a hard working staff that I supported and encouraged along the way.

When I retired from education, I did not retire from life. I went back to school and got my national certification of emergency medical technicians and later my national certification of surgical technologist. I worked in a small Oklahoma community emergency medical service as an intermediate paramedic for the next seven and a half years. Later, I chose to go indoors and worked as an emergency room tech in a local emergency department. I also went back to school. At age 59, I attended a vocational / technical program for a year and became nationally certified as a surgical technologist. The last five years of my career, I worked both in the emergency department and in surgery. Recently, I have decided to retire and spend some time with my wife as we travel, play a little golf and do some camping with our travel trailer.

As you can see, I have had multiple experiences in a variety of different careers with numerous bosses. Through observation, I have learned how to do many things well and in some cases, how to do them better. Hopefully, I can pass on in future chapters some examples of both my failures and my successes so you will not make some of the same mistakes and can pick up some good habits to enhance your own personality.

Notice I said "your own personality". It is important to accept yourself while you direct others. You can't imitate someone else as you go through life. You have to concentrate on the positive characteristics that you have in order to be your best. Be aware of your short-comings and work to make them as invisible as possible. I would be the first to state that I have made my share of mistakes in administration (some of my former teachers would be first in line to raise their hands and second that motion). The thing is, you have to put those mistakes aside and attempt not to make them again.

I know that many of you have wonderful ideas, some even better than what I might share with you in this handbook. That's why at the end of each chapter, there are plenty of blank pages for you to keep your notes and ideas. Go for it! I have not been on any mountain top to meet with a guru who has shared the secret of life with me. Maybe you have. If so, please share with the rest of us those secrets. I hope that the world would pay you handsomely for your insight. But assuming you haven't, keep your notes and ideas here so you can review them from time to time and expand upon them.

One final item before we begin. At the beginning of each chapter is a Biblical scripture that I feel relates to the ideas I am trying to address in this handbook. I think that all of us need something to encourage and comfort us as we tread the road of being a leader. For me, it was my family and my faith. It's up to you to decide what encouragements you choose to fall back on as you face your own obstacles.

The other key word in that last paragraph is "handbook." My vision for this book is relatively small, about the size of a pocket calendar. It will be something to keep handy, to keep good notes in, and to refer to as needed. Best of luck! I hope you can learn something in the following pages.

What are some of your positive personality traits that you will rely on to be an effective leader?

_____

_____

_____

_____

_____

_____

_____

_____

_____

_____

_____

_____

_____

_____

What are some of your negative personality traits that you want to change to be an effective leader?

_____

_____

_____

_____

_____

_____

_____

_____

_____

_____

_____

_____

_____

What do you hope to gain by reading this handbook?

_____

_____

_____

_____

_____

_____

_____

_____

_____

_____

_____

_____

_____

_____

Your own thoughts:

_____

_____

_____

_____

_____

_____

_____

_____

_____

_____

_____

_____

_____

_____

_____

_____

Chapter 1

REMEMBER ... YOU ARE THE LEADER!

*Now when a man works, his wages are not credited
to him as a gift, but as an obligation.
Romans 4:4 (NIV)*

"Follow me, boys!"

Take a moment and look at that word, "leader." The beginning of it contains the word "lead" for a reason. The best leaders lead through example. Great leaders lead; poor leaders direct.

An often-heard adage in the military was, "Do as I say, not as I do." Many administrators in the military were those old chiefs and seniors who went around in their dress uniforms with a cup of coffee in one hand and their finger pointing the direction they wanted you to go with the other. It's amazing that in the military, many managers often do not even have experience in the area they are managing. More often than not, rank is the most important thing. I'm not going to say those guys are not successful. I just think they have a harder time getting respect from others because they don't have the same work experiences.

Wow, isn't that an important word ... *respect*! That's what successful administrators are entitled to. It is the ultimate prize that a person can gain from someone else.

The military heroes of the past all had this same philosophy. Air Force leaders were commanding the lead bombers during many famous bombing raids. Army leaders jumped out of the plane with their squadrons. Marine leaders stormed the beaches with their troops. Navy leaders were the last to leave their sinking ships. These are stories that true American heroes will be remembered by.

There are many military leaders who are remembered for such heroic acts. Some of those who come to my mind are General "Hap" Arnold, General Dwight Eisenhower, Lt. General Holland Smith, and Admiral Chester Nimitz. All are World War II heroes who not only carried out their assignments but did so with courage, determination, and desire to make a difference in the lives of their men and the world as a whole.

Do we still have military leaders today who have this same philosophy? Consider General Colin Powell. At age fifty-two, he became the youngest officer and the first Afro-Caribbean American to serve as the chairman of the Joint Chiefs of Staff, the highest military position in the Department of Defense. During his chairmanship of the Joint Chiefs, he oversaw twenty-eight crises, including the invasion of Panama, Operation Desert Storm and the Persian Gulf War. During these events, Powell was given the nickname "the reluctant warrior" because he rarely advocated military intervention as the first solution to an international crisis; instead he encouraged diplomacy and containment to resolve the conflict.

Another modern warrior to consider is General David Petraeus. Petraeus was a well-known leader of the multi-national forces in Iraq and later in Afghanistan. In 2010, he was personally selected by President Obama and seconded by the U.S. Congress to become commander of military forces in Afghanistan. His well-known and popular leadership success earned him promotion to four-star general and he is probably the military leader best known to the American public.

I can't imagine any of these men ever complaining about the job they had to do. I am sure they relished the desire to take on the responsibility that was asked of them. They were also the type of personalities that did not relinquish their job to someone else, just in case things did not work out. I am sure these officers were on the front line, working side by side with their men and being actively involved with the success of their missions.

They took responsibility and showed their troops what it meant to be a leader. I can't think of a better legacy than to be remembered for my efforts with my fellow team members. I don't want to tell anyone how to do their job; I want to *show* them how to do their job.

These were the type of leaders that I tried to be like when I was an administrator. They were my leader heroes. My ultimate desire is to be remembered as standing side by side with my employees, not afraid to get my hands dirty, helping them to provide a successful program.

When people pass on from this life, we all want to be remembered in a certain way. We want to leave a legacy. What better legacy than to be respected for what you have done? My philosophy along these lines is, "Don't expect someone to do something that you are not willing to do yourself".

What I need to ask you before we go any further is this, "How do you want to be remembered by your family and at your job?" Just as we want to be good examples to our family, those that mean the most to us, we should also concentrate on being good examples to our staff.

I once had a class assignment in which we were expected to write an obituary of ourselves as we thought it would be written in our local newspaper. I had never done anything so difficult in a classroom before! I asked myself, "What type of legacy would I leave if I died today?" "What would my family and friends remember about me if I were no longer living?" "What successes would I be remembered for that I was able to accomplish while I was alive?" Try it yourself and see how you think your obituary would appear if you were to die today.

Write your own obituary, including what accomplishments you have had during your lifetime. How do you want to be remembered?

_____

_____

_____

_____

_____

_____

_____

_____

_____

_____

_____

_____

_____

_____

_____

Who are some individuals that you consider to be heroes that you would like to emulate as a leader?

_____

_____

_____

_____

_____

_____

_____

_____

_____

_____

_____

_____

_____

Your own thoughts:

_____

_____

_____

_____

_____

_____

_____

_____

_____

_____

_____

_____

_____

_____

_____

Chapter 2

BE CONSISTENT!

"Simply let your 'Yes' be 'Yes,' and your 'No,' 'No;'
anything beyond this comes from the evil one."
Matthew 5:37 (NIV)

**"Let's see, do I want to get up on the right
side, left side, or maybe..."**

I don't think anything destroys an organization more than being inconsistent. It creates hurt feelings, mistrust, and confusion among your co-workers.

Think about those policies that come out one day, are broken the next day, and are swept under the rug the third day. Any time an administrator puts out a memo that tells how something will be done, he should expect that policy to be followed. The last person to ignore a policy should be the supervisor.

One organization that I worked for had a shaky history of not expecting all policies to be followed all of the time. It was not that the policies were unimportant, but they were often issued out of anger concerning something that had happened when the supervisor did not know any other way to handle the situation but to put out a policy. An example of this was a policy that paramedics were to respond to all local calls that warranted a paramedic and all calls outside the city limits. Our service covered parts of three different counties and there usually was only one paramedic on duty. Unfortunately, not all calls received gave a true description of the situation going on. Some were much more severe than expected, while others sounded desperate but were nothing but a minor situation. To protect the citizens we served, a policy came out concerning out-of-town calls being answered by the paramedic on duty. Whether or not the policy was followed was determined by the paramedic on duty and often the time of day that the call came in.

One such call occurred at approximately two o'clock in the morning. The call came in and described a man who was fighting a grass fire and had received some burns to his legs. Even though the location was about five miles outside of town, the paramedic sent the other crew, who had an intermediate and a basic on the truck. I was an intermediate working as the partner to the paramedic on duty. About seven or eight minutes later, the phone rang again and the crew on scene requested that our crew respond to the call. En route to the call, I asked dispatch to place the medical helicopter on alert in case we needed transport to the burn center, approximately fifty miles away. When we arrived on scene, I opened the back door to step into the other ambulance, turned around, and requested the helicopter be launched immediately. In the back of the ambulance was a person with second and third degree burns over 90 percent of his body. His boots were the only clothing that had not been burned off. Not only had he been electrocuted by electric lines that were down, but he lay in the grass that was burning due to the electric lines being on the ground.

Did the few minutes that a paramedic was not available make any difference? Probably not, due to the severity of burns, overall body percentage involved, and the compromised airway due to the heat. Chances for survival were slim to none. However, due to the policy not being followed, this person did not have a paramedic available to administer pain-relieving medications for several minutes. Policies should be made to protect the people you serve, the people who work for you, and the organization that you represent.

That brings up a few important rules to follow:

Consider the policy before you implement it.

First, think about that policy before you put it out. Have you thought through the consequences of having such a policy? Have you worded it the way you intended for it to be perceived? Does it really say what you want to have happen within your organization? I was thankful I had a very intelligent, team-centered individual whom I depended on to bounce ideas off of before putting out a memo - my wife, someone who knows me and is sincere in wanting me to be successful.

Don't put out that policy and then ignore it a week later.

If you change your mind and decide that what you were thinking won't work, don't be afraid to come back and say "Hey, I messed up!" Let folks know that what you wanted to do isn't getting accomplished. By simply ignoring your mistake and leaving the policy out there, you are setting yourself up for failure the next time you put out a policy. Your co-workers will think, "Don't worry about it; he will change his mind (or forget about it) in a week." If you really want to be taken seriously, then either stand by your decisions or let folks know when you change your mind.

Don't be influenced by every Tom, Dick and Harry.

You've heard the saying that some folks just like to "blow smoke under your skirt"? Well, let me tell you, not all breezes you feel under that skirt are natural. Believe it or not, there are folks out there who are out for the betterment of only one person … themselves! They sit around the office, laugh at all of your jokes, and tell you what a terrific job you are doing. All the while, they try to influence you into doing something that might be terrific for them, but terrible for your organization. Be careful with whom you hang your hat. Make sure they are sincere and want what's best for your fellow co-workers. If you don't, you will soon find yourself out on a limb, and no one is going to get a ladder to help you down.

Avoid favoritism.

The same goes for those guys who seem to get all of the extra benefits of the job. Be careful not to be so painfully obvious with giving the same folks any benefit that comes along. These might include recognition, promotion, or extra pay due to overtime being available. Yes, hard working folks deserve to get rewarded when possible. But, when they get their cake, and get to eat it too, you are creating jealousies that can't be corrected, hurting both the boss and that special employee.

I once heard a fellow employee tell our boss, "You just don't like me anyway!" I really don't think that was the case. Unfortunately, there was a lot of favoritism going on at that time, and I think because of it, the employee only got it partially right. The underlying problem was that with so much open favoritism, the employee *felt* that the boss didn't care for her. Irreparable damage can result from staff members who don't feel appreciated or given the same opportunities as other employees.

Consider carefully your policies before you put them out to be followed. Are you willing to see that they are followed? Are you willing to support your staff when they follow the policies and are you willing to deal with staff when they do not follow them?

Under what circumstances would you consider "ignoring" a policy?

_____

_____

_____

_____

_____

_____

_____

_____

_____

_____

_____

_____

What steps would you follow to implement new policies within your organization?

_____

_____

_____

_____

_____

_____

_____

_____

_____

_____

_____

_____

_____

Your own thoughts:

_____

_____

_____

_____

_____

_____

_____

_____

_____

_____

_____

_____

_____

_____

Chapter 3

IF IT'S IMPORTANT, HE'LL SAY IT AGAIN!

"'Consider carefully what you hear', he continued. 'With the measure you use, it will be measured to you – and even more.'"
Mark 4:23 (NIV)

"Did he say something?"

Communicating with each other is something that man has tried to deal with since recorded history. It began with such primitive methods as someone beating on a log or drum, and progressed to smoke signals, and then to using a shiny object to reflect the sun's light in a particular direction. With the invention of papyrus and primitive ink, man was able to save what he wanted to pass on to someone else in a more permanent method.

In 1837, William Cook and Charles Wheatstone patented a telegraph which worked by electromagnetism, so people were able to communicate over long distances. Almost forty years later, on March 10, 1876, Alexander Graham Bell finally succeeded in speaking a few words on a telephone with which he had been experimenting. In another room, his assistant, Thomas Watson, waited for the test message. Suddenly, Bell spilled some acid from a battery on his clothes. He cried out, "Mr. Watson, come here. I want you!" Bell had invented the first successful telephone.

Today, technology has progressed greatly and we are able to communicate in much more sophisticated ways. We can now use instant messages, emails, and satellite telephones that can be used from virtually anywhere on Earth.

Technology has changed, but a person's ears have not really improved much to receive information through the years. We still have selective hearing or are desperate for information to be passed on to each other. Communicating to one another with information or instructions is essential in assuring success of an organization. Besides that, people have a tendency to get a little frustrated when they don't know what is going on that affects them.

There's a fine line between successful communication and harassment. As an administrator, I could have met with my staff weekly and passed on pertinent information to them. However, if I had asked them to meet with me weekly, they would not have appreciated me infringing upon their after-school hours. A little creativity and a variety of techniques kept my staff from giving up their time but allowed me to pass on information that I considered important.

One of the things I did to keep frustrations at a minimum was to write a weekly newsletter for my staff and leave it in their mailboxes. Not only did it give me a chance to pass on important information, but it also was instrumental in "patting staff members on the back", and sharing motivational quotes and messages.

To get feedback from my staff, I preferred to meet with small groups during school hours by providing assistants to cover classes while we met. That way, we were able to share ideas and be on the school's clock. Any business can use the same idea to deal with select employees.

When it was necessary to meet with an entire staff, there were three rules I felt needed to be followed:

1) Start your meeting at the time you tell your staff you are going to start.
2) Keep it brief. Go over your materials and give time for feedback.
3) Keep those after-hours meetings to a minimum.

By keeping to those three rules, I was telling my staff I appreciated them and their time. Not only that, but if my staff knew I promised to follow these rules, they were more willing to be on time and prepared when I was ready to start.

How important is it to get information out to the folks who work for you who are truly in the "trenches"? All of us have been in situations where we do not feel we have been given the entire picture of what was going on. How did you feel about that situation? I've been there myself. I felt like I was not important enough to be included in the selective circle of influence. I also felt frustrated that I could not do my job properly because I didn't have the knowledge needed to be successful. Not only did that hurt my chance of success, but our business's chance of success as well. As an administrator, you need to let your folks know as much information as is feasible regarding what is going on. The information you get back from them could be beneficial to your organization's success and make your job much easier at the same time.

What ideas do you have about passing information on to your workers?

_____

_____

_____

_____

_____

_____

_____

_____

_____

_____

_____

_____

_____

How important is it for workers to "hear" the information you are telling them? What are some of the obstacles you need to overcome?

_____

_____

_____

_____

_____

_____

_____

_____

_____

_____

_____

_____

_____

_____

Your own thoughts:

_____

_____

_____

_____

_____

_____

_____

_____

_____

_____

_____

_____

_____

_____

Chapter 4

THE TWO MOST IMPORTANT WORDS TO RAISE MORALE: "GREAT JOB!"

"But blessed are your eyes because they see,
and your ears because they hear."
Matthew 13:16 (NIV)

"I am so awesome!"

In an August 30, 2010 Gallup poll it was reported that 51 percent of Americans report very little recognition for good work. That statistic took me back a bit when I first heard it. As I thought about it more, I realized that not only was it accurate, but according to statistics, was growing. That statistic, as well as the next one I will share with you, has to do with a very important word we throw about a lot these days ... *attitude.*

All of us carry around an attitude with us on a daily basis. Sometimes, that attitude is positive and sometimes it's negative. I've heard professional people call it "carrying your own weather."

There are a lot of things that affect my attitude when I go to work. My attitude might be due to a disagreement with my family. It might be because I had finally achieved a goal I had worked hard for and was proud that I was able to accomplish. Or, it just might be that I don't want to face the attitude of other people at work, whether it is my co-workers, or even my boss. Whatever the case may be, it brings to mind another statistic from the same August 30, 2010 Gallup Poll: 70 percent of workers report they are more productive when they are around positive people.

Another interesting people poll comes from a January 5, 2010 *New York Post* survey. It found that only 45 percent of Americans are satisfied with their work. There were several reasons listed as to why this all-time-low statistic was happening. Among them were that people did not find their jobs interesting, incomes were not keeping up with inflation, and health insurance cost more. Two even more interesting reasons were that there was no sense of teamwork in most work places anymore and that bosses don't take time to listen to workers' ideas and acknowledge workers' difficulties on the job. Feedback from the survey even went so far as to say that bosses need to come down to the employee level more and see what is actually going on in the work place versus only paying attention to what paperwork is telling them is happening.

So what does that have to do with you, boss? Well, I think you, as the administrator, are very much responsible for the atmosphere your people work in. People will often mimic the attitudes at work that you foster. If you come in with a poor attitude, the people who work for you will probably develop a poor attitude themselves. If you come in, happy to be at work and looking forward to a successful day, chances are that your co-workers will also. Positive attitudes are usually contagious!

So as the boss, what can you do to promote positive attitudes? Well, think back to that first August 30, 2010 Gallup Poll statistic we began this chapter with. Don't be afraid to let folks know that you appreciate their efforts. Take notice when others do a good job. Let them know that you are aware of it. Often times, it means more to that individual when you are one-on-one and just pat them on the back and tell them, "Great job on that project you just finished". Other times, you might share with everyone that a person or a group went above and beyond the call of duty on a particular activity. Finally, don't be afraid to recognize *everyone* and let them know they are appreciated. I used to send out personal notes to both employees and my students' parents.

One of the more difficult situations that I inherited when I became a principal was unruly students attending ball games. Students were unsupervised, running around, and disturbing other people who were supporting our extra-curricular activities. Some students I had to send home to get their attention. On a more positive note, I encouraged my staff to help me look for students who were sitting and cheering for our athletes during the games. On Monday, I would send personal notes home to parents thanking them for helping me make sure their children follow school rules at ball games. I also would put in our weekly newsletters the names of kids who were recognized for their behavior at the games and thanked them for showing their "Tiger Pride" (our school mascot).

As a principal, I also tried to encourage a private, staff meal several times a year. I usually provided and cooked the meat, and asked others to provide the rest. We not only got to enjoy a great lunch, but had some wonderful fellowship while doing it. I also would do corny things like purchasing 100 Grand candy bars for each of my staff. I would take the candy bar to each staff member and let them know they were worth that much money to me. Yes, it truly was corny, but most people really appreciated it.

The most creative thing that I ever did for my staff was an idea I got from the story "All the Good Things" from the original *Chicken Soup for the Soul*. It's the story of a teacher who had her class think of the nicest thing they could say about each of their classmates and write it down. That weekend she wrote down the name of each student on a separate sheet of paper and she listed what everyone else had said about that individual. One of those students was a young man named Mark. Later, Mark was killed in Vietnam and at his funeral, his parents showed the teacher the note that Mark had gotten with all his classmates' comments. He carried it with him wherever he went, even to the day he died. They told her how much Mark had treasured this project.

I did the same thing with my staff. Luckily, I had a computer to help me compile all the comments and statements they had to share with one another. Still, it took several weeks to complete my project. When I finished it, I printed it on a piece of decorative paper and gave it to each staff member as a Christmas gift. To the day that I retired, I often saw these notes had been framed and put on the wall behind the desks of many of the staff members. I know how much they appreciated the effort I had made. I hope they saw how much I appreciated them.

So, why is keeping that positive attitude important in the work place? Well, other than being more productive, there are two other things I feel it accomplishes. Both of these things have to do with how you are seen as an administrator. First, an administrator will only be as successful as the people who work for him. Remember, they are the ones who do all the hard work in the trenches and make you look good! Second, don't expect others to support you unless you support them. People will never take chances unless they know they are supported and are encouraged to learn from their mistakes.

Progress is made from making mistakes. I can't help but think of what Thomas Edison said about all the mistakes he made when trying to invent a long-lasting light bulb filament. "I have gotten a lot of results! I know several thousand things that won't work!" Who knows what type of light bulbs we would have today if he had quit after only a few attempts. Be aware that there are times that mistakes will be made. Support your staff when those mistakes are made and let them know that mistakes should not be an excuse for turning down a challenge in the future.

You've taken the effort to support your staff. You recognize the importance that your staff makes in your organization. You let them know how much you appreciate their effort. Still, there are people who work for you who are not happy and they have a negative influence on your organization. What are you prepared to do now?

The first thing I would encourage you to do is to look closely at the situation. Be honest with yourself and see if you have done anything to contribute to the situation. Have you been consistent with your expectations and the way you have treated this individual? Does the employee feel that you have consistently shown favoritism to other workers and he has not gotten his recognition for the work he does? Does that employee contribute to the overall success of your organization, or does he contribute to negative attitudes of your other employees? Finally, consider the legal ramifications of taking action against this employee.

After completion of this self-examination, you need to determine a course of action to follow. Begin by discussing the situation with your employee. Make sure he is aware of what is going on and the results of his attitude. Evaluate what he has to say and be open to suggestions he might have to correct the situation. Does your employee's response offer legitimate concerns that you need to consider?

Set some time limits in which you want to see changes made. Look for changes of behavior, not particularly a change of attitude. There are times that you simply cannot change a person's personality, no matter how good a manager you are. You simply want to change how these personalities are affecting your work place. Consider giving this individual a special assignment he is capable of performing. Hopefully, this will make him feel more of a team player. If you see no change or improvement in your negative employee, consider taking action against him. We will discuss this in more depth in the following chapter.

What are some ideas you have about things you can do to recognize your staff members?

_____

_____

_____

_____

_____

_____

_____

_____

_____

_____

_____

_____

How would you deal with a member who has a negative attitude that affects the work place?

_____

_____

_____

_____

_____

_____

_____

_____

_____

_____

_____

_____

_____

Your own thoughts:

_____

_____

_____

_____

_____

_____

_____

_____

_____

_____

_____

_____

_____

_____

Chapter 5

KEEP IT LEGAL

*"Does our law condemn anyone without first hearing
him and finding out what he is saying?"*
John 7:51 (NIV)

"Bad boys, bad boys,
what ya gonna do …"

Perhaps some of you are thinking by now that a leader's obligation stops at just being an example. Not quite true. Yes, I very much believe we need to be showing our employees what it means to be dedicated, hard- working individuals. But, there are times when you have no other alternative, and disciplinary action should be put into effect.

There are a few things I would put into the category that it is necessary to immediately terminate an employee. The first thing I would put into that category is stealing. I'm not advocating that you fire someone for taking an ink pen or a box of staples. I'm saying that someone who is guilty of embezzlement or taking of pieces of property that are a detriment if lost by a business would probably fall into that category. Let's not put a price on this item, although some of you might try to do just that.

Another item in that category might be to intentionally and maliciously try to hurt the business or a co-worker. When people come to work, they want to feel like they are safe from harm, both physically and sexually. Physical and sexual harassment cannot be tolerated within the work place.

Finally, how about a person who refuses to do the job he was hired to do? I have seen too many folks who begged to get into a system, told the boss they would do "anything" to be hired, but then changed their minds and didn't want to "get their hands dirty" doing what they were hired to do. That just isn't appropriate. I was involved in one such termination process. When I was an elementary administrator, I hired a bilingual teacher assistant to take care of a young Hispanic student who was born with spina bifida. Her responsibility was to ride the bus with the student both morning and afternoon. During the day, she stayed with the girl and took care of all her needs. Although she was only responsible for this one student, I made sure that she received her appropriate breaks and lunch period that all my staff was entitled to have.

This went on for a full year. The assistant did her job and proved to be a valuable asset to our school. The next year, the assistant came in and told me that she needed to be reassigned; she wanted to work with other students, even though there were no other positions available. No other assistant wanted to "trade" positions with her. Although she had it specifically in her contract to work with this student with special needs, had signed her contract and had proven to be a valuable employee, she now refused to do the job she was hired to do. Even with the documentation we had available, it was a difficult process to terminate this assistant. Fortunately, we were able to dismiss the assistant and hire someone else to take care of our special needs student.

These are just three categories I would consider appropriate for immediate termination. Perhaps you and your fellow administrators would like to make up your own lists and let your folks know that such actions would not be acceptable.

Then we come to the person who is in a position, and he struggles getting the hang of things. That is a situation where the administrator needs to have some leverage and some patience helping him become more proficient in his job. Look especially at the attitude of the person who is struggling. Is he unsure of his performance? Is he afraid of making a mistake? Would assistance from you or another co-worker help him get the hang of his job? *Does he want to do a good job?* There is a big difference between someone who is really wanting and trying to do a good job and someone who just doesn't care. I would do what I could to keep someone with a positive, caring attitude in my employment as long as possible. As mentioned in our previous chapter, there are lots of folks out there who just don't seem to care about the job they are doing.

Even then, you might come to the point that you have to terminate someone's employment for either not caring or being physically / mentally unable to perform his duties. When it comes to that, remember to *keep it legal*.

There are three rules of terminating someone's employment:

1) Document; -
2) Document; -
3) Document.

Paperwork is one of those necessary evils that come about when you finally decide termination has become a necessity.

The first thing I would suggest is that you become aware of your local system's / business's policy. Every business should have a policy manual that describes the termination process. Follow it carefully. Do not deviate from it, or just "look for something that would fit your situation". That is the best way of getting yourself or your business into legal problems.

There are also state requirements when it comes to fair practices and the termination of employees. For example, every employee should have a personnel file. Anything placed in that personnel file should be shown to the employee. Every employee has the right to answer any issues that are placed in his file. That doesn't mean he has to sign a reprimand or notice of termination. That simply means that you offer him the chance to sign and have a witness available if he refuses to sign what you want to place in his file. Above all, you must give him the right to answer any charges or notices that you would like to place in his file. Don't forget, when you place something in a person's personnel file, make it look professional. Don't hand scribble a note accusing someone of something and place in his file. Remember, every document that is placed in that file has the potential to be a piece of evidence in a court hearing. Also, don't forget to date those documents and have all required signatures on them.

It's up to you to know what state laws govern your particular situation. If you have questions, contact a lawyer or the state Department of Labor to get them answered. The old saying, "Ignorance of the law is no excuse" is quite appropriate under these situations. Be aware, not only of your rights as an employer, but also the rights of your employees.

Are you aware of any of your state's laws that would affect worker's rights?

_____

_____

_____

_____

_____

_____

_____

_____

_____

_____

_____

_____

_____

What characteristics differentiate between a person who is struggling to do his job and someone who doesn't care?

_____

_____

_____

_____

_____

_____

_____

_____

_____

_____

_____

_____

_____

Your own thoughts:

_____

_____

_____

_____

_____

_____

_____

_____

_____

_____

_____

_____

_____

Chapter 6

PROVIDE A SERVICE TO THE PUBLIC AND REMAIN A PROFESSIONAL WHILE DOING IT

"To slander no one, to be peaceable and considerate, and to show true humility toward all men."
Titus 3:2 (NIV)

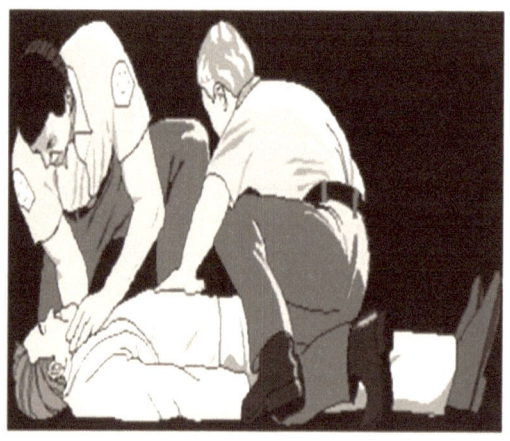

"Not on my watch, you don't!"

Have you ever gone into a store to purchase something, only to find the person waiting on you has an attitude that they are doing you a favor by selling you that item? We sometimes forget that we are here to serve the public, whether we are selling something or just providing a service. Most jobs are in the world today not only to make your life better, but to make the lives of others better.

I think most sales people do not realize what a difference they make with the attitude they demonstrate. Personally, I would rather do without, or even pay more for an item and get it from someone who is showing some courtesy. As a culture, we have forgotten that the customer is always right. That doesn't mean you can walk out with a free or greatly reduced-price product. It simply means that you ought to feel like you are getting your money's worth when you leave that store. If all of us were waiters and waitresses, how much money would we have in tips at the end of the day? If part of our salary were dependent upon our attitude, would we be rich, or out looking for another job?

The same thing goes with the service or program that you work for. Most of us work for the public in some way. It is extremely important to act professionally when you are around the people you serve. That goes for the boss, as well as the employees. I used to remind my staff that it's not enough for you to think of yourself as a professional. You have to look professional, act professional and be professional for people to consider you a professional. If your staff or you don't think the public views you in a professional way, perhaps you need to seriously look at your business to see what the public is seeing to get that attitude.

The way your workers or your workplace looks establishes a first impression for the public that is often difficult to overcome. Would you go to a dentist whose outward appearance reminds you of a packing-plant butcher? Not only is having blood on your uniform or scrubs dangerous and unhealthy, but it creates a bad impression that your customer cannot forget. The same goes with the workplace. If your office space is open to the public and it's unorganized and dirty, or gives the impression that your customer is not welcome, that is the way you will be perceived.

What about the way you and your employees treat or talk to each other while doing your job? It's one thing to have a little fun with each other when it's just you around, but what happens if someone from the public comes in at an inopportune time? If they see that attitude, will they think you can provide them with the service they expect? Be careful with your language, attitude and behavior if the public can see those things without your knowledge.

Once again, as the boss, it's up to you to establish that proper professional attitude. Not only is it your job to show the desired attitude, but you can't be afraid to make some changes to get your desired results.

Remember:

Look professional.

Act professional.

Be professional.

How do you think the public views your business / organization?

_____

_____

_____

_____

_____

_____

_____

_____

_____

_____

_____

_____

_____

_____

What can you do to improve the way the community views you and your organization?

_____

_____

_____

_____

_____

_____

_____

_____

_____

_____

_____

_____

Your own thoughts:

_____

_____

_____

_____

_____

_____

_____

_____

_____

_____

_____

_____

_____

_____

_____

_____

Chapter 7

NEVER STOP LEARNING

"Do your best to present yourself to God as one
approved, a workman who does not need to be ashamed
and who correctly handles the word of truth."
2 Timothy 2:15 (NIV)

"If A = B and B = C, then …"

Does a person ever get to a point in his life that he feels he has learned all he needs to know? That point in his life is probably when he just died!

Think for a moment about how much knowledge has increased over the past twenty years. Think about all of the new inventions and improvements to the things we use on a daily basis. I can remember the first computer I bought back in 1985. It had 64K of memory. When I bought some more memory and doubled that to 128K, I thought it had more memory than I would ever use. As you probably know, that is not enough memory to even start a program you would buy today.

I have read that the computer used to land Neil Armstrong and Buzz Aldrin on the moon in 1969 had no more memory than most of the hand held calculators we have today. So, what does this have to do with the price of tea in China? Well, how can we not improve our organizations and keep up with modern technology and yet hope to still survive? We will find ourselves losing business to our competition and eventually we will be out of business altogether.

In the Preface I mentioned that I worked for seven and a half years as an intermediate paramedic in a small Oklahoma community. I can tell you that advances in medicine continue on a monthly basis. Unfortunately, too often people get in a rut and depend on knowledge they learned years ago. We often don't want to keep up with advances, sometimes because of cost and sometimes because of fear of change. We justify that by saying things like, "Well, what was good years ago when I started is good now." No, it is *not*! Lives are sometimes lost because of that attitude. What can be of more value than someone's life, which is taken away far too soon? In any business, whether it be medicine, education, sales, or whatever…learn to do your job better through technology and new procedures to make our lives and the lives of the people we serve better.

I faced that same attitude when I was an administrator in school systems. Change is simply difficult to face. We feel unsure and insecure about what those changes might bring. But, one of my most favorite sayings is, "If you continue to do what you have always done, how can you expect to get something different than what you have always gotten?"

Try an exercise before we go any further. Put this handbook down and fold your arms across your chest. When you have done that, try folding them the other way, with the other arm on top. How does it feel to you? For most of us, it's a little uncomfortable and we had to think about how to even fold them the other way. Some can't wait to get back to the way they normally fold their arms. This is just an example of the emotional discomfort that people have when dealing with changes. Perhaps it can be just as irrational as this exercise.

How do you direct change within your organization? The first thing you should do is put yourself in the shoes of the person who is resistant to changes. Assure him that you understand his hesitancy and that change is suggested to improve the way you have done things in the past, not to completely replace the important work that has been accomplished previously. Assure your staff that you will keep them informed of how things are going along the way. Be prepared to justify why these changes are taking place. Provide for input from your staff and listen to what they want to share. Above all, demonstrate that you value the people this affects the most and appreciate their efforts.

Never settle for the norm, especially if there is a better way of doing something. One word of warning, don't be willing to change and jump into a different swimming pool every day. As we have already discussed, being consistent is important also. But if you find something that will improve your business, keep a professional attitude, and help make your employee's job easier and better, don't be afraid to go for it.

Just keep telling yourself … change is good, change is good. Also, be prepared for some resistance.

What is the most difficult change you have ever faced? How did you approach this change?

What changes do you see that would improve performance in your organization?

_____

_____

_____

_____

_____

_____

_____

_____

_____

_____

_____

_____

_____

Your own thoughts:

_____

_____

_____

_____

_____

_____

_____

_____

_____

_____

_____

_____

_____

_____

_____

Chapter 8

THE BUCK STOPS HERE!

*"Brothers, each man, as responsible to God, should
remain in the situation God called him to."*
1 Corinthians 7:24 (NIV)

HARRY S. TRUMAN
The 33rd U.S. President
1945–1953

"STOP!"

President Harry S. Truman had a sign on his desk in the Oval Office that simply said, "The Buck Stops Here". It comes from the slang expression "pass the buck" which means that you are passing the responsibility on to someone else. It originated from poker, in which players used a marker (originally a buckhorn-handled knife) to show whose deal it was. By passing the "buck", a player simply chose not to deal and allowed the next player to deal the cards.

I think "Give-'em-hell Harry" had the right idea. He knew that as president, he ultimately had the responsibility and did not pass the blame on to someone else. I can only imagine the responsibilities he had on his shoulders after taking over following the death of Franklin Roosevelt near the end of World War II, as well as the decision to drop the atomic bombs on Japan.

Isn't taking responsibility for your actions a refreshing attitude for any politician or anyone else in the role of responsibility to have? As a boss, it's important for you to keep that thought in the back of your mind. It says a lot about you during a time of difficulty or how you handle controversy.

Pick up any book and you will find hundreds of leadership styles. They range from the far right where the boss is almost a dictator, to the far left where the boss is just someone with a name plate on his desk. Remember at the beginning of this handbook, I told you it was important to be yourself in your leadership style? That doesn't mean you can't pick up some good ideas from others to improve your own leadership style.

We all have seen movies where the boss is a total jerk and sabotages everyone to work his way up the ladder. That's the guy who takes credit for all the good stuff and blames others for all the bad stuff that happens. There are a couple of movies I would like to mention here, *9 to 5* and *Office Space*. If you have not seen these movies, I don't want to ruin them for you, but I think some things are relevant and are worthy of mentioning. I would encourage you to watch the movies at some point in time.

The movie *9 to 5* is the story of three ladies who all work in the same huge company, Consolidated Companies. When their lives and futures are thrown together due to extenuating circumstances, they realize they have one thing in common, a very deep dislike for their sleazy, chauvinistic boss, Franklin Hart Jr. After a series of fantasies and desires to "kill" their boss, the ladies actually think they have poisoned Hart by accidentally poisoning his coffee, only to have him walk in the next morning because he never drank the coffee the previous day. While discussing the day's events in the bathroom, the ladies are overheard by the office snitch, who goes and blabs it to Hart. Mr. Hart threatens to call the police and have the ladies arrested. To prevent him from doing that, the ladies kidnap Hart and hold him hostage in his own home. The women then use the occasion of the boss's absence to effect numerous changes around the office as they hide the reason for his disappearance from the other workers. Things seem desperate when Hart's wife finds him when she returns from vacation early; the ladies' plan appears bound to fail. Along comes the company's chairman of the board, impressed with the changes he assumes Mr. Hart implemented and wants him to move to Brazil to work in the company's local operation. In the end, the ladies find happiness and Hart is abducted by an Amazon tribe, never to be heard from again.

My favorite character in *Office Space* is Milton Waddams, a meek, fixated collator who continually mumbles to himself about his workmates and about setting fire to his workplace. All Milton wants is a few simple comforts at work, a nice desk, a piece of cake at a co-worker's birthday party and his red Swingline stapler. The truth is that Milton was actually laid off five years earlier, but a computer malfunction continued to let him receive a paycheck. Once the malfunction is fixed, his bosses don't tell him that he has been fired and just assumes that he will eventually leave when he doesn't get paid. For most of the movie, Milton is abused by many co-workers, especially his boss, Mr. Lumbergh. After having his office cubicle moved on several occasions, he ends up in the cockroach-infested basement. Milton finally snaps when Lumbergh takes his beloved red stapler. He ends up burning down Initech, disappears with its money and eventually gets back his red Swingline stapler from another disgruntled co-worker.

I do not advocate any of the actions of the characters from these two movies. However, it does bring up a humorous consequence of events when you deal with people who are frustrated and angry at work. The severity of their actions is a result of that person's character and attitude. It's up to you, boss, to handle the controversy that results from these employees.

I always told my two kids when they were growing up that you have people in this world who see other people as "better" than they see themselves. When that happens, one of two things will occur. Either that person will work to get himself up to the other person's level, or he will work to get the other person down to his level. I hope you can see this attitude of bringing others down to their level is not good for trust, morale, or the betterment of a business.

On the other hand, there are organizations that do everything (promotions, pay raises, and recognition) by way of committee. People get together and make a group decision on most aspects of the work place. The problem with that is that when things fall apart, no one is there to take the blame or to extend a ladder to the boss out on that limb. It's *nothing* but a popularity contest! Important circumstances such as longevity, ability to do your job, and accreditation should be extremely important factors in making those decisions.

That's where you, as the boss, come into play. Don't get me wrong, when it came to hiring individuals, I often asked people they were going to work with to sit in on the interviews. I requested and appreciated input from them in making the decision. However, I also felt that it was my responsibility to check into their past work histories and to contact those references listed on a resume. Ultimately I made the decision which I passed on to my school board as to who I felt would do the best job.

A good friend in my district used to tell me, "That's why you get the *big bucks!*" It also was his way and my way of saying, "*the buck stops here!*"

Be honest with yourself: How well do you handle controversy at times of difficulty? What can you do to be more proficient?

_____

_____

_____

_____

_____

_____

_____

_____

_____

_____

_____

_____

_____

_____

_____

What leadership style do you think you have?

_____

_____

_____

_____

_____

_____

_____

_____

_____

_____

_____

_____

_____

_____

Your own thoughts:

_____

_____

_____

_____

_____

_____

_____

_____

_____

_____

_____

_____

_____

Chapter 9

EVEN GOD RESTED SOMETIMES

"By the seventh day God had finished the work he had been doing; so on the seventh day he rested from all his work."
Genesis 2:2 (NIV)

"Man, this is the life!"

For those of you who believe in Creationism, that verse should be an important one for you to comprehend. After all He had created in six days, God took a rest. If you don't believe in Creationism, but you do believe in God, it's just as significant that you realize even God rested. My point is, if God rested at some point in time, why would it be unusual to think that occasionally, we need to "chill out" as well?

No one who has never been in an administrative position can recognize the pressure that is on a person who has the welfare and success of people and a business in his hands. When you make a decision, it affects so many people and so many aspects of a job. It's more than just one person making one decision about only one thing.

In short, the mental stress that comes with making executive decisions takes a toll on a person's mental and physical well-being. Short-term complications include headaches, high blood pressure, stomach ailments, and emotional outbursts. Long-term complications are generally much more severe and longer-lasting, including heart attacks, strokes and major organ failure.

Of course, stress can be handled differently by different personalities. Some people revel with stress in their lives. They love the excitement that comes with the adrenalin rush (like so many of us who work in the emergency medical field). Other people just seem to enjoy "messing" with other people.

For the most of us who truly want to do a good job, we worry that the decisions we make are the right decision at the right time. We also worry about the effect those decisions cause in the long run. It's like throwing a rock into a pond. There's a big splash, but in the long run, the ripples that flow out from that point will eventually affect the entire surface of that pond. Every bit of surface area of that pond will be affected by those ripples.

Is it any wonder that a person needs to occasionally let go and get away from the working environment? I find it amazing how many people in the emergency medical field are divorced. Some of that has to do with people having to work a variety of jobs because the pay for EMT's and medical techs is just not that good. They are never at home. Another reason is that they take the stress of the job home with them. They can't have a normal husband / wife relationship because they can't get away from work stress.

Two things I feel are important to maintain a "normal" family environment would include you making sure you enhance family time when you have it. I enjoy going places when my wife and I have time off together. We can go out and eat together, go camping, or just spend some quiet time at home together.

Secondly, find some time just for yourself. What you do is up to you and what you enjoy doing. For me, it's playing golf, or doing some wood working. For others, it can be whatever you enjoy doing yourself. The best things are those that take your mind away from the working environment and what is going on at the time.

To make a long story short- to improve your own personal health and the health of your family relationships, take some time to get away from work and work on building those other extremely important relationships. This includes your family relationships, as well as those personal relationships that you have in your own mind and body. In the long run, your head, your heart, and your body will thank you for your efforts.

What do you enjoy doing to "get away from it all"?

_____

_____

_____

_____

_____

_____

_____

_____

_____

_____

_____

_____

_____

_____

What things are most important in your life? List them in order of importance:

_____

_____

_____

_____

_____

_____

_____

_____

_____

_____

_____

_____

Your own thoughts:

_____

_____

_____

_____

_____

_____

_____

_____

_____

_____

_____

_____

_____

_____

Chapter 10

WHAT HAVE I GOTTEN MYSELF INTO?

*"Here is a trustworthy saying: If anyone sets his heart
on being an overseer, he desires a noble task."*
1 Timothy 3:1 (NIV)

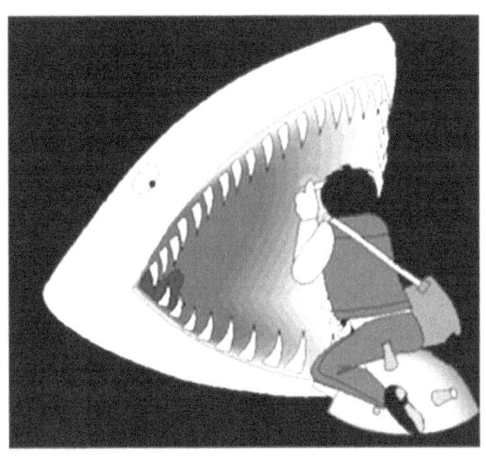

"Open up and say, 'Ahhhhhh'"

63

Everyone has his own reasons for becoming an administrator. It is important for those who want to be a boss to be honest with themselves and come to their own conclusion as to why they are choosing that particular avenue.

Why do you want to become an administrator? Some people might have a wonderful story behind why they choose this field. Other reasons might not be so practical. Let's start with some examples that probably are not the best reasons to become an administrator.

One reason some people want to become a boss is the money aspect. I would be naïve to not agree that money was originally an important factor in my decision to get a degree in administration. After all, I was a young father who wanted to provide for my children and give them many of the extra things in life that I could not otherwise provide for them. Earning an extra $10,000 per year was quite an incentive. When I did become an administrator, it became quite clear the extra money came at a great price. When you figured all the additional overtime that was required to do my job, all of the baby-sitting services I provided by attending so many ball games and other extra-curricular activities, as well as the meetings with school and civic organizations that I held, I'm not sure the hourly wage was that much more. This doesn't even take into consideration the headaches, irritable colon spells, or the anxiety that came with the job. No, if money is your sole decision for becoming the boss, you definitely are in store for failure.

How about the thrill of being able to tell someone what to do? Well, if you haven't figured out already that we shouldn't tell folks how to do their job but instead *show* people how to do their job, then perhaps you need to start with the Preface and read to this point again. Success and productivity are measured by the people who work for you. You don't get those things by bullying or trying to force people to be happy in their jobs.

What rationales are important to be a successful administrator? One of the earliest we talked about was getting respect from others. There's not a greater reward we earn than to earn respect from others.

It all has to do with that legacy we leave when we are no longer a part of the organizations we work for.

I also think there is nothing more satisfying than the pride you feel when others recognize your efforts to be a good boss. Self-esteem and inner satisfaction cannot be matched when you know you have helped others to be successful or completed an extremely difficult project. Have you ever done something that no one thought was possible to accomplish? Wow! There's not a better feeling of pride that a person can have.

How about having that same feeling by helping someone else accomplish one of those difficult projects? Not only do you feel great about it, but so do they! J.C. MacAulay once said, "One of the marks of true greatness is the ability to develop greatness in others."

I hope you take some time here to put what's on your mind into the "Your Own Thoughts" section that follows. Answer these important questions… Why do you want to become a boss? Why do you want to become a better boss?

Why do you want to become a boss?

_____

_____

_____

_____

_____

_____

_____

_____

_____

_____

_____

_____

Why do you want to become a better boss?

_____

_____

_____

_____

_____

_____

_____

_____

_____

_____

_____

_____

_____

_____

Jim Willis

Your own thoughts:

_____

_____

_____

_____

_____

_____

_____

_____

_____

_____

_____

_____

_____

Chapter 11

MAKE A DIFFERENCE
TO SOMEONE TODAY

*"I have fought the good fight, I have finished
the race, I have kept the faith."*
2 Timothy 4:7 (NIV)

"You can count on me!"

We have covered a variety of ideas to make you a better boss and able to make a difference in other people's lives. Yes, there are lots of other things that we could cover. No, you can't be a better boss by becoming Jim Willis or anyone else. At the beginning of this handbook, I mentioned that it's important for you ultimately to retain your own personality. What's important is for you to recognize your own short-comings and try not to make the same mistakes over and over again. It's also extremely important to recognize your strengths in management and take advantage of those aspects of your personality.

There are two things I would like for you to think about. The first thing is that there are many, many more books out in the publications world as to how to be a better boss. The purpose of this handbook is to get you to go back to thinking in a practical, common-sense sort of mind-set. We often times want to make things just too complicated. When I go out and play golf, if I try to think of too many things at once, I will not enjoy playing, nor do very well. Are my hands right? Am I addressing the ball properly? Am I swinging at my hips? How's my follow-through? At some point in time, you were probably in the shoes of those people who are working for you now. How did you want to be treated? What type of respect did you want to receive? Is it difficult to think that we just need to treat our employees with the same respect and appreciation we expected when we were in their position? You don't need to read a hundred books to get that concept.

Secondly, you can't be someone else and be successful. That doesn't mean we don't make ourselves as successful as we can be. That doesn't mean we don't learn from our mistakes. What that does mean is that we take our best qualities and try to utilize them to be a better boss. It is so important to continue to mention that we learn from our mistakes. We all know those mistakes are out there. We all know we will make them. The important thing is to learn from those mistakes.

I like to mention that a child will only touch a hot stove once to know it is hot; he doesn't need to touch it again to recognize that fact. Have you ever seen a child touch a hot stove over and over again to see if the stove is really hot? Once usually does the trick!

I think we need to get back to some good old-fashioned values and common sense. Bosses need to learn to take care of their staff. We need to get along with each other. Confidence in the people who work for you is a must. A positive attitude by workers who want to do a good job will go a long way. People who want to put in a good day's work for a good day's pay have been all but lost at times. The most important thing is… *you*, as the boss, are the one who ultimately is responsible for the morale and success of your organization. Be the example you need to be. Be the difference in the lives of those who work for you.

I wish you luck in your endeavors!

What qualities would you look for in the people who work for you?

_____

_____

_____

_____

_____

_____

_____

_____

_____

_____

_____

_____

_____

As a boss, what is your responsibility to the people who work for you?

_____

_____

_____

_____

_____

_____

_____

_____

_____

_____

_____

_____

Your own thoughts:

_____

_____

_____

_____

_____

_____

_____

_____

_____

_____

_____

_____

_____

_____

_____

Chapter 12

MOTIVATIONAL QUOTES

*"Therefore encourage one another and build each
other up, just as in fact you are doing."*
1 Thessalonians 5:11 (NIV)

**"One of these days I'll be famous, and you
will remember what I told you!"**

Don't expect someone to do something that
you are not willing to do yourself.

Carry your own weather.

Look professional.
Act professional.
Be professional.

If you continue to do what you have always done, how can you expect to get something different than what you have always gotten?

The Buck Stops Here!

When you have people in this world who
see you as "better" than they see themselves,
one of two things will occur:
1) They will work to get themselves up to your level; or
2) They will work to bring you down to theirs.

Carpe diem!

... (Latin for "Seize the day")

"When you allow the emotional weaknesses of others to control your circle of influence, you empower those weaknesses to control you."

Stephen Covey

"One of the marks of true greatness is the ability to develop greatness in others."

J.C. MacAulay

"Even though you are on the right track, you will get run over if you just sit there."

Will Rogers

"There are three kinds of men. The one that learns by reading. The few who learn by observation. The rest of them have to pee on the electric fence for themselves."

Will Rogers

"Never, Never, Never give up!"

Winston Churchill

"Success consists of going from failure to failure without loss of enthusiasm."

Winston Churchill

"Success is simple. Do what's right, the right way, at the right time."

Arnold Glasow

Your favorite quotes:

_____

_____

_____

_____

_____

_____

_____

_____

_____

_____

_____

_____

_____

ABOUT THE AUTHOR

*"Therefore, as we have opportunity,
let us do good to all people, especially to those
who belong to the family of believers."*
Galatians 6:10 (NIV)

"The Willis crew"

After graduation from high school in 1971, Jim Willis joined the United States Air Force, serving a tour in Oklahoma, a year in Southeast Asia, and one in California. He got out four years later as a staff sergeant. He continued to stay in the Air Force Reserves in Midwest City, Oklahoma for the next nineteen years, retiring as a master sergeant. The main reason for getting out of active duty was to go to college, where he earned a BSEd in elementary education, a MSEd in reading, and certification above his masters in elementary administration, all at the University of Oklahoma. Jim spent the next thirteen years as an elementary teacher in two different districts. He was able to begin his career in administration after that, becoming an elementary administrator, where he spent the next thirteen years in a single school district in Southwest Oklahoma. When he retired from education, he did not retire from life. Instead, Jim went back to school and got his national registry certification and worked in a small Oklahoma community emergency medical service as an intermediate paramedic for seven and a half years. At 59 years of age, he once again went back to school and received his national certification as a surgical technologist. For the next five years he worked in a local hospital as an emergency department tech and a scrub tech in surgery. This is his first book.

Jim recently retired and lives outside of Norman, Oklahoma with his wife of forty years, Jan. They have two children, Ryan and Caleta. Ryan is an officer in the United States Air Force. Caleta left the Air Force and is currently attending the University of Oklahoma. Jim and Jan are members of the Highland Church of Christ in Tecumseh, Oklahoma.